THIS
BOOK
BELONGS
TO

Love
Yourself.

Everyday is
a new
beginning.

Life is what happens
when you are busy
making other plans..

John Lennon

LIFE IS A PROCESS
OF BECOMING,
A COMBINATION OF
STATES WE HAVE TO
GO THROUGH.
ANAIS NIN

LOTUS: purity and devotion

TREE
OF
LIFE

SHINE LIKE A STAR

Butterfly Beauty.

Everyday is beautiful!

A loving heart is the beginning
of all knowledge.
Thomas Carlyle

TWO HEARTS THAT BEAT AS ONE.

GRATITUDE

Every rose has it's thorn.

Create a
SACRED
SPACE

You change your
life by changing
your heart.
Max Lucado

Hibiscus Flower-Circadian Cycle
The Flower of Hawaii

Made in the USA
Columbia, SC
24 October 2023

24907894R00035